CHILDREN'S DE... Y0-CFS-837

LET'S MOVE

MEMPHIS/SHELBY COUNTY
PUBLIC LIBRARY AND INFORMATION CENTER

Gift of
Robert & Kaye Hiatt

LET'S MOVE

Enjoyable Physical Activities and Games
for Children between the Ages of 3 and 7

FROM THE CELLAR TO THE LOFT

Bulky rubbish and unwanted furniture is piling up everywhere from the cellar to the loft – oh dear! But in the sports hall, out of the chaos comes …

Meyer & Meyer Sport

Editor: Heidi Lindner, Pipo-Lernwerkstatt, Neumünster, Germany
Authors: Gisela Stein, Heidi Lindner
Illustrations: Silke Mehler
Translation coordination: Gisela Stein
Translated by Jean Wanko

From The Cellar To The Loft/Ed. by Heidi Lindner
-Oxford: Meyer & Meyer Sport (UK) Ltd., 2003
(Let's Move)
ISBN 1-84126-125-4

All rights reserved, especially the right to copy and distribute, including the translation rights. No part of this work may be reproduced – including by photocopy, microfilm or any other means – processed, storedelectronically, copied or distributed in any form whatsoever without the written permission of the publisher.

© 2003 by Meyer & Meyer Sport (UK) Ltd.
Aachen, Adelaide, Auckland, Budapest, Graz, Johannesburg,
Miami, Olten (CH), Oxford, Singapore, Toronto
Member of the World
Sports Publishers' Association
www.w-s-p-a.org
Printed and bound by **FINIDR, s. r. o.,** Český Těšín
ISBN 1-84126-125-4
E-Mail: verlag@m-m-sports.com
www.m-m-sports.com

Publisher's Statement

The games and exercises described in this book have been tried and tested many times, without any problems, by the authors and the children in their care. However, teachers, parents and any other adults using this book for source material must ensure that the children in their care play within a safe and secure enviroment. The publisher cannot be held liable should accidents occur. Correct and standard procedures on health and safety should be followed at all times.

Contents

Dear Readers 6

Pieces of Usual and Unusual Small Apparatus 9
Let's Go: With a Bounce and a Brolly but no Rain. . . 10

More Small Apparatus 17
My... Your... Our Handkerchieves 18
For Towels and Feet 21
And now Your Hands 27
Cuddly Cushions 31
Big Boxes 45
Gymnastics with Big Telephone Books 51
Over Tables and Chairs 59
The Crazy Waiting Room 60

Large Apparatus – Moving Scenery 69
Balancing – Is Everything Well-Balanced 70

Small Games 81
The Washing Pegs Tower 82
Egg Boxes 83
Everyone Plays against each other
– Everyone together 84

Fun Activities 85
A Day out with the Family in the Land
of the Game Inventors 88

Creative Corner 93
A Child's Snuggly Cushion Costume 94

Dear Readers,

Every child knows its own home and is well familiar with every nook and cranny throughout the house. We all know what we might find there: lots of rooms, where furniture, washing, crockery and other useful things we need every day are stored away.

Tables and chairs are everyday objects which we use without thinking about them; but we're not often allowed to use them as gymnastic apparatus. You'll be amazed to discover all the things you can do with these bits of furniture.

And – would you believe it – the cushions are still on the settee, once very useful for our pillow fights, but from now on they'll not only be used as flying objects, but as keep-fit apparatus and things to look for, as well as being disguised and carried around.

But we've not only been having a look round the living quarters of the house, we've also had a good hunt through the boxroom to see if we can find anything ideal for playing and doing gymnastics with: planks for balancing on, old catalogues and thick books, egg boxes, large boxes and packing cases have turned up, making us think how all this junk can make our sports sessions more interesting and varied.

The results of all our reflections appear in this edition of "Let's Move", which also includes the programme for "A Day out with the family in the Land of the Game Inventors", as well as a detailed report on the subject of balancing.

We wish you lots of fun as you embark on all the games in "From the Cellar to the Loft".

Gisela Stein, Silke Mehler and Heidi Lindner.

PIECES OF USUAL AND UNUSUAL SMALL APPARATUS

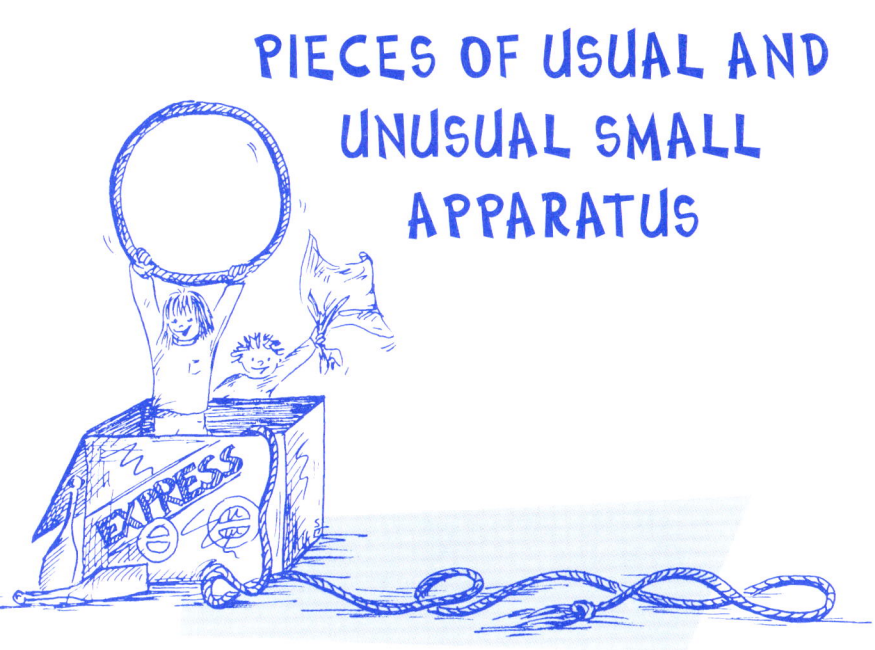

You can increase your range of available apparatus in the sports hall by everyday materials because:

- they cost little or nothing and are easy to obtain.
- they can be brought in to the gymnastics session by the families concerned
- they are familiar to the parents and the children
- they arouse the children's imagination and creative skills, as they discover and learn how to use the materials
- a wide variety of sensory impressions and types of movement is made possible by the different structures of the materials
- they make a change from other gymnastics sessions
- the kind of movement games practised in the sports hall can easily be developed further at home
- they can steer against our consumer-oriented behaviour

Umbrellas, of course, belong to our unusual apparatus.

LET'S GO: WITH A BOUNCE AND A BROLLY BUT NO RAIN

There are lots of families with a good stock of old umbrellas – big family umbrellas, telescopic umbrellas and children's umbrellas – and it's just these that we're going to play with. But before using these in the sports hall, everyone must be made well aware of the dangers of using them as toys and group leaders should ensure that there is plenty of space for all manoeuvres.

SPINNING UMBRELLAS

Everyone tries to spin their umbrella like a top.

We'll put all the umbrellas up in different places for you round the hall. Now – can you manage to set them all spinning at the same time?

WIND MACHINES

See how much wind you can catch in your umbrella with it up. How could you push the wind away from you again e.g. by holding your umbrella open over your shoulder, or whilst you run fast or by pushing your umbrella in front of you?

HIDDEN

All the umbrellas are put up in various places round the hall. Can you manage to hide underneath them, so that nothing of you is visible at all?

The children have hidden behind their umbrellas. Then, so that the group leader can guess who's behind which umbrella, the children can stretch out an arm or a leg etc. so that it can be seen.

Umbrella Jugglers

See how many umbrellas you can carry at once e.g. on your wrists or ankles or under your chin. Who's got a good idea for balancing one or two umbrellas on some other part of their body – like maybe balancing closed umbrellas on your hands, knees or on the back of your neck?

Joined By Two Brollies

Try either in pairs or small groups to hook your closed umbrellas together. How can you then move around the room without losing touch with each other? E.g. run round in pairs, one child lying down is pulled around by another child, make a roundabout together or turn fast or slowly.

Rain child

All the children run about round the sports hall with their umbrellas closed. Two children play at being the rain child. They've hooked their umbrellas together and can only move forward together. The rain child tries to catch the other children and to put them on a specially-prepared mat. Once two children are on the mat, they become the next rain children, and hook their umbrellas together ready to go catching. This continues until there are only rain children running round.

Umbrellas with extra materials

MATERIALS: table-tennis balls, sandbags, tennis balls, balloons, beer mats, cotton-wood balls, corks, scarves

Work out for yourselves different ways of carrying the various materials in the material pool, from one side of the hall to the other without dropping any of them.

Each child puts various small objects in its umbrella and then they all try to pinch things from each other's umbrella.

Each child is set up with something to throw and then they all make an alleyway. One child runs down the alleyway with its umbrella up, acting as a shield against the various missiles as it tries not to get hit by anything.

Again, one child runs down the alleyway with its umbrella up. This time, though, the other children try and throw their objects into the moving umbrella.

Whilst still up, the umbrellas are filled with tennis balls, table-tennis balls or balloons. The umbrellas are then spun so fast that some balls or balloons fly out. Who can manage to twirl their umbrella so fast that nothing is left inside it?

Working in pairs or groups, and with your umbrellas open, try playing hurling and catching small objects backwards and forwards across the hall.

Umbrella Darts

Some umbrellas are hung up at different levels on the parallel bars, and the children then see how they can throw various small objects from a distance away into the umbrellas.

A Feeling Umbrella

The umbrellas are filled with certain things, ensuring that there are at least two the same in each umbrella. Then the children feel all the objects with their eyes shut and try to find the same.

Decorated Brollies

Which umbrella looks the most attractive?

Brightly-coloured scarves, present ribbons or crêpe paper can be knotted round the edge of the brollies.

Lay a length of material, a large sheet of paper or mosquito net across each brolly, so that the child underneath can't be seen.

Then go for a walk with your decorated brollies, or walk without touching anything, or strut about, or turn your brolly around on your shoulder, or greet other passing children. Could you manage all that whilst walking along a catwalk? (i.e. bench)

MORE SMALL APPARATUS

Do you only use handkerchieves for wiping your nose or mopping up tears, and are towels only used for drying your hands? Of course not! Handkerchieves bring a bit of variety into our movements and let the children make new discoveries about different materials. Added to which, towels are ideally suited to bringing our feet into the forefront of one of our movement sessions.

I'm sure you've never seen anyone putting gloves on before using a towel! So there's no reason to keep your shoes and socks on when you want to play, with your feet and a towel. Come on then, let's see those feet out of their woolly and leather containers and let's get on with some tricky footwork!

MY... YOUR... OUR HANDKERCHIEVES

Here are a few handkerchief exercises for you, where throwing and catching are particularly important, because their flight is slow and the hankie has a large area to catch hold of.

Hold a hankie in your hand and wave energetically with it using big arm movements – you can stand still, or run forwards and backwards.

Throw your hankie into the air and then catch it on different parts of your body – hand, arm, knee, shoulder, head, back, bottom..........

Now work with your partner: throw the hankies high into the air and catch your partner's hankie.

Working in groups of four, throw all the hankies into the air at the same time and catch only one of them. Use different, funny ways of catching the hankies as they fall to the ground.

Discover various "nose-cleaning contortions" e. g. from behind with your legs apart.........

Put a hankie on your arm, your tummy or your chest and then run very fast, so that your hankie sticks to that part of your body when you've reached a certain speed.

And what about when it's on your head?

Trap a hankie between your feet and wave it in the air, as you lie on your back.

Keeping the hankie between your feet, rock on your back.

Hold the hankie between your feet and stretch your legs into the air as high as possible.

Still with the hankie between your feet, go round and round with your bottom as a roundabout.

Sit on a hankie but without touching the floor with any part of your body.

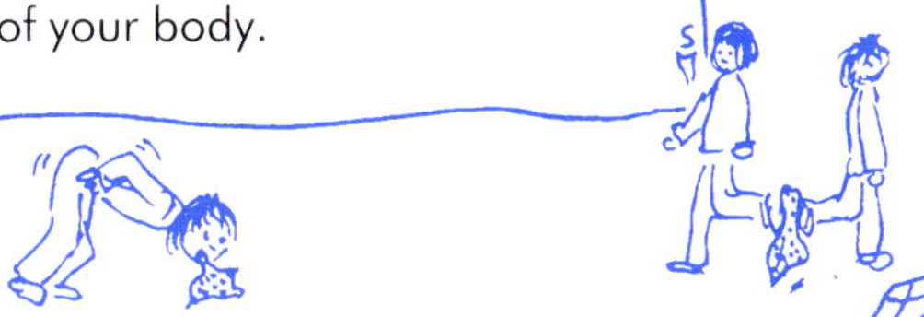

All this will have made your hankie very dirty, so let's take it to the washing machine. This can be made out of a tyre or a circle of rope or an imaginary rope.

Pick your hankie up with your feet and carry it to the washing machine.

This is where the hankies are rubbed, scrubbed and rinsed.

Our arm does all the rinsing work by making big circles with the hankie in front of and next to our body.

There are now various ways we can dry the hankies:

- if the weather's fine – spread the hankies out from one hand to the other and blow them dry.

- if the weather's bad – grab hold of the hankies at two opposite corners, and twist them in front of you until the hankie's rolled up tightly. Pull it apart again quickly and let it twirl round by itself.

Finally, the hankie must be ironed and folded up tidily.

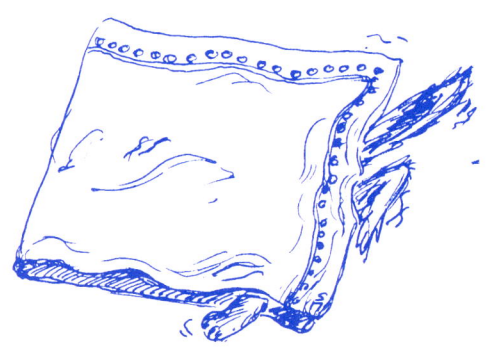

For Towels and Feet

 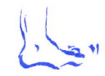

Whoever thinks that towels can only be used for drying dishes is surely mistaken!
A towel can be an ideal toy, with which you can set your body in motion, using your fantasy and creativity.
Let's start with your feet, because we'll now show you how well towels can be used for playing with your feet.

Everyone will need either an old guest towel or a large cut up bath towel, so that it's not too rough or heavy for little feet.

The children sit on the floor

The children ▬ put their towel in front of them on the floor, push it around with their feet and then stroke it until it becomes smooth again.

The children ▬ push the towel together with their feet and then put their feet on it, so that no more of the towel can be seen.

The children ▬ pull their legs up towards them, put their feet on the towel and then wipe the floor with it, backwards and forwards and from left to right.

The children ▬ claw the towel with one set of toes, lift it in the air and cover their other foot with it.

The children — hold the towel tightly with both feet and, pulling their knees up towards their chest, travel in a sitting position on a roundabout.

The children — hide both feet under their towel, then put their right (or left) big toe in the air to make a bump.

The children — hide both feet under their towel and wriggle their toes.

The children — hide both feet under their towel, spread their toes out and then claw them in again.

THE CHILDREN STAND UP

The children — stand on the towel and dance "The Twist".

The children — stand on the towel and crumple it together with their toes.

The children — fold the towel with their toes and spread it out again.

The children — clamp the towel between the toes of their right or left foot and then hurl it up into the air.

TWO PARTNERS PLAY TOGETHER

Both children — push, hurl or slide their towels to each other with their feet.

Partner 1 — makes a gateway, through which Partner 2 can push his/her towel.

Partner 1 — covers his/her partner's feet without using his/her hands; then swap over.

The children — sit opposite each other. Partner 1 clamps the towel between his/her feet, goes round in a circle on his/her bottom and then passes the towel to Partner 2's feet.

25

Both children — sit about 50 cm apart, back to back. Partner 1 clamps the towel between his/her feet, rolls onto his/her back and then passes the towel in the air to his/her partner's feet, who has also rolled onto his/her back.

The children — sit opposite each other, each holding a corner of the towel. Then, like a sort of tug-of-war, each tries to pull the towel towards them.

The children — take it in turns to rub each other's feet with the towel.

 ... AND NOW YOUR HANDS

Your feet have now done enough work and deserve a long rest. Now it's time to let your hands do some work as they can help the towels find lots of more new things to do.

They can turn into:

A flying carpet — take hold of the towel on its shorter side and let it flap about over your head as you run around fast.

A waving flag — either let the towel wave about slightly (a light wind) or flap about fiercely (a strong wind).

A plane — slide forward on your tummy on the towel with your arms stretched out sideways.

A helicopter — run round the room, swinging your towel around in a circle.

A roundabout — two children each take a corner of the towel and run round and round each other.

A rowing boat — sit on the towel and push yourself forwards or backwards with your feet.

A train — stand on the towel and slide forwards with your feet. Several children standing in a row could make a long train.

A garden fence — one child, bent over, holds the towel horizontally in front of itself.

Another child climbs over it or creeps underneath it.

A temporary path — all towels are put on the ground at varying distances apart, so that the children can run slalom round them. The children could also hop from stone to stone or try and go along the path, without stepping off the stones.

A hiding-place — some children lie down close to each other, and are then covered with all the available towels. Who can recognize his/her friend's hand just peeping out from underneath a towel?

Big washing day — all the children kneel close together in a big circle with all the towels in the middle. By pushing all the towels along first to the left and then to the right, you can simulate washing the towels in a washing machine.

Then, by pushing them fast in the same direction, they are spun dry.

Flying objects – all the towels are thrown into the air and, with a bit of luck, caught again with a particular part of the body.

When you've reached the point, where the children don't have any more ideas to try out, all the towels are carefully collected together, folded and put in a pile.

Cuddly Cushions

What's that?

It's small, light and cuddly. All children love it and many of them often carry it around the house with them. You can put your head on it and sit your bottom on it. It can fly through the air and goes "plop" when it lands on the ground again. It doesn't even hurt you, if it lands on your nose. You can make different shapes out of it and beat it and sometimes it even has a name.

Yes, you've guessed it right – we're talking about a cuddly cushion. This is an ideal piece of apparatus for our children and it's allowed to come with us today into the sports hall. There it's going to get the surprise of its life, because it´s quite remarkable what we can find to do with it.

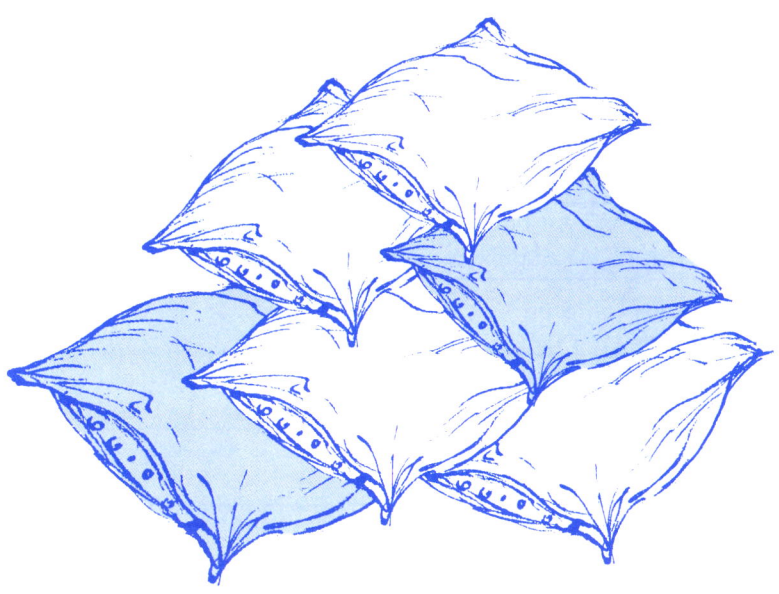

The Cuddly Cushion Parade

Materials: A cuddly cushion about 40 cm^2 for each child.

Cuddly Cushion Obstacle Race

Spread the cushions out evenly round the hall. The children then move about to "running" music, which you can stop from time to time, giving the children the chance to complete the following tasks:

 Whizz round all the cushions.

 Go round each cushion in order and then run to the next.

 Run over the cushions.

 Hop forwards, backwards and sideways on and off the cushions or jump right over them.

 Hop on one leg over the cushions.

 When the music stops, touch as many cushions as possible with various parts of your body (hand, nose, tummy, bottom, knee etc.).

 Stand next to a cushion, supporting yourself on it and try to turn round in a squatting jump!

 Make a bridge (high press-ups) over the cushion each time the music stops.

Each time the music stops, stand on one leg on the cushion, like a stork among the lettuces!

CUDDLY CUSHIONS — FLYING OBJECTS

Take the cushion and

 throw it as high (far) as possible.

 throw it away from your body and catch it with both hands (or on another part of your body).

 throw it up high so that it turns round in the air.

 throw it backwards through your legs apart.

 throw it backwards over your head.

 hold it at chest height with both hands, let it go and catch it again before it reaches the floor.

 throw it high into the air and try and clap your hands, before catching the cushion again.

 throw it high into the air, turn round on the spot and then catch it again.

 push it forwards with your foot.

 two children throw their cushions at the same time, aiming to hit the other cushion in the air.

34

Cuddly Cushions — Keep Fit Apparatus

First lie on your tummy with the cushion just in front of your head, then pass it from one hand to the other behind your back.

Kneeling on the ground, push the cushion forwards as far as possible and then back again. (You can also do it from left to right)

Trap the cushion between your feet and then play roundabouts (go round in a circle on your bottom).

Trap the cushion between your feet, take your feet over your head, put the cushion down and then bring it back again.

Sitting on the floor, put the cushion down in front of you and beat it hard with both feet.

In a standing position, let the cushion circle round your body — round your waist, then round your neck, legs etc.

Two children lie down on their tummies a short distance apart and pass their cushions across the floor to each other.

Cuddly Cushion Transportation

The cushion

- is carried on the palm of your hand, as you walk or run forwards or backwards.

- is balanced on your head.

- is carried with arms outstretched high above your head.

- is balanced on your neck, with you bending forward slightly.

Now walk on all fours, carrying the cushion on your back.

Carry the cushion on your tummy, as you walk like a spider.

The cushion is then trapped between your knees, after which you hop backwards or forwards with it.

Two children trap one or two cushions between various parts of their bodies and then move together forwards, backwards or round and round in a circle.

CUDDLY CUSHIONS — LOOKING FOR OBJECTS

PARTNER 1 — lies on his/her back, hides a cushion underneath him/herself;
PARTNER 2 — then tries to pull it out. (swap roles)

PARTNER 1 — hides the cushion under his/her clothes;
PARTNER 2 — looks for it and tries to pull it out. (swap roles)

PARTNER 1 — sits on the cushion;
PARTNER 2 — tries to pull partner 1 off it. (swap roles)

TWO CHILDREN — hide a cushion and then take turns in looking for it somewhere in the room.

(All the cushions should look different for this game, which you can achieve by threading different coloured bits of wool through the cushions or sticking coloured spots on them.)

Cuddly Cushions — Building Materials

All the children make a road together out of all the cushions; or, alternatively, a slalom course or a wall, in which they can move about.

All children use the cushions to make a picture e. g. a teddy, a house, a snake, a car etc.

All the children build a high tower out of the cushions. They then take it in turns to jump or fly over this tower, with a bit of help from the leaders. (hold each child under the arms and take hold of its upper arm)

All the children build a cosy corner, where you can play finger games or tell exciting stories.

Cuddly Cushion Fight

All the children throw cushions at each other.

Cuddly Cushions Dressed Up

To suit this particular theme, we've had some costumes made for our cuddly cushions, with which you can turn ordinary cushions into a sun, moon, clouds and stars and then find all sorts of new ways of using them. But they don't only come in useful as cushion covers, you can do lots of other things with them as well. For example, it occured to us that they don't only fit the cushions, but are also ideally suited to our children when we want to divide them into groups for team games. These new children's play outfits can easily be made by helpful parents using the instructions for "little shirts" in our Creative Corner.

Today we're going to dress our cuddly cushions up in their new costumes and then play with the sun, the moon, the clouds and the stars:

1) All the children run about round the hall with their cushions, then the group leader or one of the children calls out a symbol from one of the cushions, and the children with that symbol sit down quickly on their cushion.

2) All the children run about round the hall with their cushions and when a particular symbol is called out, only the children with that symbol stand still and throw their cushions into the air as high as possible. One after another, suns, moons, stars and clouds take it in turns to fly through the sports hall.

3) The sun is now at the centre of our activity. All the suns try and stay close together in a tight group protecting each other against the cushions being thrown by the other "symbols". After a while the turmoil ends and the children run about all over the hall until another symbol is called out and battle recommences!

4) The sky looks stormy today and this storm is driving everything else in the sky along with it. By making strong hurling movements with their cushions, all the "cloud" children drive the suns, moons and stars round the hall. Each of the "cloud" children tries to touch as many other children as possible with its cushion.

5) The sun meets the moon, the clouds meet the stars. Carrying on like this or in other combinations, you can make pairs or small groups, who play together with their cushions. You'll find that a lot of the cuddly-cushion games described in the previous chapter are suitable for this.

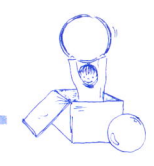

6) Sometimes there's a lot of turbulence in the sky. The stars, moon, sun and clouds seem to be having a big argument. Because none of them can speak, they use bumping down on the earth to vent their anger. All the children hold their cushions over their tummies and then, working in pairs, crash into each other with their upholstered tummies.

7) Some road-building is going on in the sky. There's a sunshine street, a starry road, a cloudy path and a moonshine path. The cushions are sorted out and set out in long rows with about 20 cm between each cushion. You can then organize the following tasks:

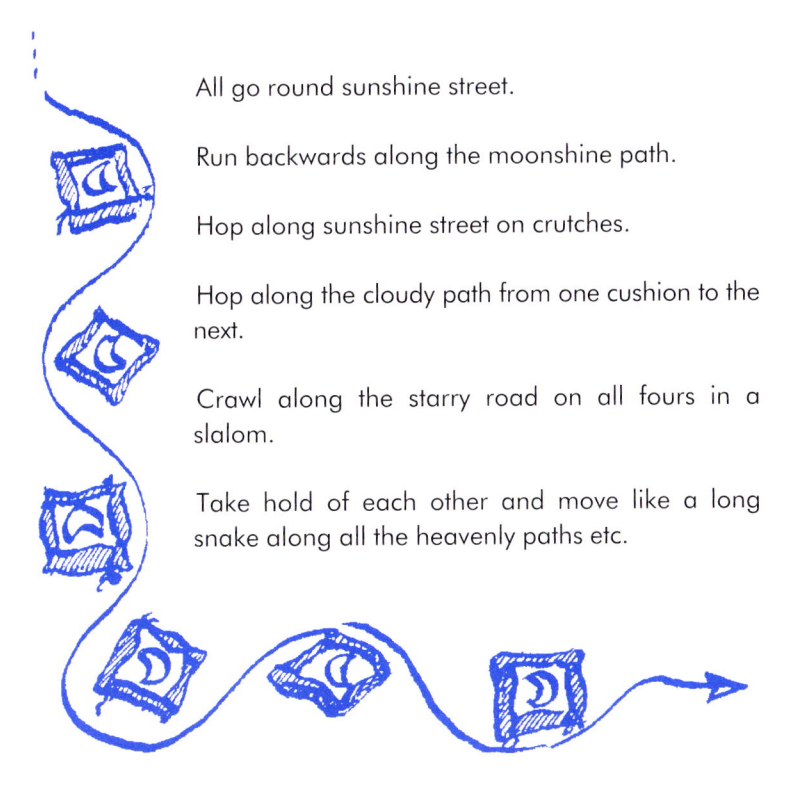

All go round sunshine street.

Run backwards along the moonshine path.

Hop along sunshine street on crutches.

Hop along the cloudy path from one cushion to the next.

Crawl along the starry road on all fours in a slalom.

Take hold of each other and move like a long snake along all the heavenly paths etc.

43

8) Finally, all the children can make a beautiful picture of heaven with their cushions. There's a big sun, made up of several little suns, a big fat moon (also made out of several moon cushions), lots of individual stars and clouds.

Big Boxes

Oh dear, what a boring day! Nobody wants to play with us! Yet again dad and mum do not have any time for us, because they`ve decided to do some important work and, as always, we children are only in the way.

Suddenly, we hit on a great idea: we'll rummage around in the spare room; there are bound to be some exciting things to find in there. Off we go! Yes, just as we expected, here are some of the best toys you could wish for. Just look over there – the big packing cases from our last move and the boxes from our television set, the computer and the frig. Now let's see what we can do with all this!

45

Gymnastics with Big Boxes

Everyone takes a box and:

- carries it in front of his/her tummy.
- carries it high above his/her head.
- pushes it forwards with his/her hands.
- sitting on his/her bottom, pushes it with his/her feet.
- walking on all fours, pushes it with his/her head.
- pulls it behind him/herself whilst walking backwards.
- rolls over the sides.
- opens the end of the box and crawls through the tunnel.

WITH A PARTNER

- the children run round the hall in pairs and, when the music stops, one child crawls into a box, the other one stays outside and sets up a drumming concert on the box. After another run round, they swap over, so that all the children can hear what the drumming sounds like from inside the box.

- when the music stops, one child disappears into the box and the other tries to push its crate of freight across the room or, alternatively, to ride with the "freight" as a roundabout.

- One child covers their eyes, so that they don't see which box their partner has hidden in. Once all the children have disappeared, who wanted to hide, their partners come and look for them. They keep knocking on the boxes, asking the hidden children to make some noise or other. The hunters will recognize their partners by the various squeaking and giggling noises.

Additional materials

As well as the boxes, bean bags and tennis balls are put out. Out of the boxes you can make goals

- for throwing things at.

- for throwing things into.

- for rolling balls into their side openings.

- for knocking over when you've piled them up on top of each other.

THE WHOLE GROUP

- All the boxes are lying evenly spaced out on the floor with an opening at one side. All the children run around to some suitable running music. When the music stops, they try and disappear into a box as fast as they can.

- Some boxes are taken out of the game, so that there isn't a hiding-place for everyone. Who can find an empty box, when the music stops? Do you think two children or more could squeeze into the same hiding-place?

- All the children run around the room and, whenever they pass a box, they knock on it with their fingers, the palm of their hand or with both fists.

- A catching game: put out between four and six boxes depending on the size of your group. One catcher (or in big groups 2 or 3) tries to tick a child. The children can escape to the safety of a box before they're caught, but must come out again as soon as the catcher has gone away.

- Working together, the children can make a fortress or a house, where they all move in together and sing a song or play a finger game.

Gymnastics with Big Telephone Books

We've by no means come to the end of everything in the spare room which we can use for hurtling and rollicking about with. Piled up from the floor to the ceiling, there's a stock of yellow books. Who do you think has put them there? Lots and lots of old, forgotten telephone books are sitting here collecting the dust. Telephone books?

Can we really do gymnastics with them? Let's take them and some ancient mail order catalogues off into the sports hall and see what we can do:

Our all sorts' library

All the books lie spread out round the room.

The children — run round all the books.

The children — take a running jump over all the books.

The children — do a finishing jump over the books.

The children — jump on one leg over the books.

The children — slap each book they pass.

The children — stand on a book and jump off it backwards.

The children — run on all fours round one book at a time.

Book gymnastics

Everyone has a book:
The children — push the books across the room as hard as they can.

The children — carry their books on their heads, on their backs (walking on all fours), on their tummies.

The children — working on their knees, push their books as far forward as possible and then back again.

The children — push their books out to the left and the right, still working on their knees.

53

The children — sit on the floor, put their books on their thighs and spin round on their bottoms like a roundabout.

The children — from a crouching position, take the book round their body.

The children — push the book under their outstretched legs.

The children — turn the book through 360° with their feet.

The children — from a crouching position, turn over a few pages.

The children — lying on their tummies without any elbow support, turn over a few pages.

The children — lying on their backs, put a book on their tummies and watch the book go up and down as they breathe in and out.

Book street

All the books are lying on the floor in a row with spaces in between.

The children — go from one book to another.

The children — jump from one book to another.

The children — run a slalom race through the books.

The Bookworm

The children — stand in a long row one behind the other. The books are gradually put onto this conveyor belt and passed along from one hand to the next. There´s a high tower at the end of the conveyor belt. Is it stable enough for the children to stand on at the end?!

Books in the Tunnel

The children — stand in a long row with their legs apart and the books are passed through their legs.

The children — build high bridges next to each other, so that the books can be pushed from one section of the bridge to another with only one hand.

The children — build a low bridge (backward press-ups) and again with only one hand, push the books under their backs.

THE BOOK TOWER

Some children stand on a book and try to pile up as many books as possible under their feet, without touching the floor.

Other children keep on passing them more books. (then swap over)

Some children stand on a book and, whilst the children do a little jump, other children put another book on the pile.

Some children stand on one leg on a book then, and whilst they hobble other children try and put more books on the pile. (swap roles and legs!)

All the children try and build a book tower under their feet, finally balancing a book on their heads.

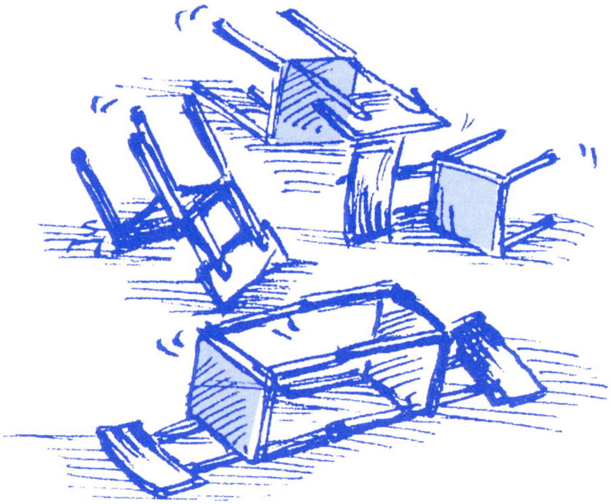

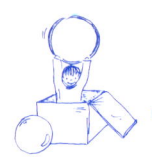

OVER TABLES AND CHAIRS

You're not allowed to sit still in my waiting room. The tables and chairs don't have to stay in the same place all the time; you can push them about just as you like and, if you've got clean shoes on, you can even do your gymnastics on them as well.

THE CRAZY WAITING ROOM

However, not everyone who likes to play and do gymnastics with children has a well-equipped sports hall at their disposal. Sometimes you'll only find a room to move about in with a bench and a few mats. But, at least you'll usually have plenty of tables and chairs. So let's have a look and see what we can do with all these alternative bits of gymnastic equipment.

There are some most unusual noises coming out of Dr. Turner's waiting room today. From behind the door you can hear rumbling and thumping about, sounds of happy laughter and funny squeaks. As we get a bit closer, we can see the following sign:

> No sitting still in my waiting room.
> The chairs and tables musn't stay in the same place.
> You can move them about and,
> If you have clean shoes on (or take your shoes off),
> You can even do gymnastics on the furniture.

Full of curiosity, we open the waiting room door a little bit and peep in to see what all these "not-so-ill" children are getting up to.

A LONG LINE

Lots of chairs have been put in a row facing alternatively in opposite directions (like musical chairs).

Children hop with their feet together from one chair to the next.

Children balance on the balls of their feet over the row of chairs (giant´s walk).

Children creep along like cats on all fours from one chair to the next.

Children crawl under the chairs as if through a tunnel.

The children are now parachutists, as they climb onto the chairs and, when told to, they all jump together onto the ground.

THE CHAOS

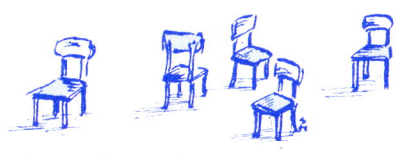

All the chairs are spread out all over the room.
The children run about round all the chairs on all fours like little dogs. When the music stops:

- they crawl into a kennel (under a chair)

- they sit begging on top of a kennel putting their "front paws" on the backs of the chairs

- the little dogs drum on the chair backs with their "front paws"

- they lie down quickly (on the ground) in front of a chair and drum on the seat with their feet

- they sit down quickly on a chair and kick their feet about

All the children are transformed into planes and, accompanied by a suitable song, they fly through the streets in the town (round the chairs). They finally land on their tummies on the seats of the chairs.

The children grab hold of each other and make a long snake. The snake's head then pulls them all in a slalom round the chairs or/and underneath the chairs.

A MAZE OF CHAIRS

The chairs are set out next to each other to make a maze with their backs facing in lots of different directions.

The children try and find their way through the maze and

- clamber over all the chair backs.
- crawl under all the chairs.

One child manages to find its way through the maze of chairs, so it lays a trail behind itself with a length of wool. A second child follows this woolly trail and thus clambers along the same route as its partner.

Each child is given a blown-up balloon and tries to play the balloon higher and higher into the air, whilst making its way through the maze of chairs.

Two children wriggle across the seats of the maze trying to shake hands with each other as often as possible, but not across the backs of the chairs.

BACKWARDS AND FORWARDS ALL OVER THE PLACE

Put the chairs in any way all over the room e. g. sideways, lying down, upside down etc.

The children then see how they can get through all this chaos. They try and find holes to crawl through and hurdles to get over.

NOW, HERE COMES A TABLE AS WELL

Who lives upstairs and who lives downstairs?

Two or three tables are now put out amongst the chairs and the children move about round them all as quickly as possible. When the group leader calls out "upstairs" or "downstairs", the children must find a suitable object or human being they can either scamble underneath or climb on top of.

The children can please themselves how they tumble around depending on whether they hear "downstairs" words e. g. elephant, worm, daisy, cellar, caterpillar, mouse etc. or "upstairs" words e. g. roof, sky, cloud, plane, helicopter, butterfly.

Tip: if you see all the children trying to climb onto the same one or two tables for "upstairs", then put out a few more tables to avoid accidents.

Going Up- and Downstairs

By putting chairs sideways round a table, you can quickly make a staircase. If you have lots of children, make several staircases to avoid queueing.

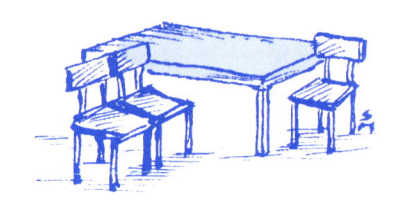

The children can then discover lots of ways of getting upstairs on their own or with a friend, and then of coming down again on the other side.

Here are a few ways of doing it: forwards on all fours, on your knees, on tip-toe, crouching, twisting round on the first stair, going through the space between chairback and seat, backwards on all fours feet first, working with a partner – one forwards and the other backwards etc.

The Jumping Table

By putting down a mat or mattress to jump onto, you can jump off this table and fly through the air.
Whilst doing this, the children try:

- to stretch out into the air as high as possible.

- to turn round in the air, so that they're facing the table again when they land.

- to pull their legs up as they fly.

- to aim to jump and then land at a certain point, e. g. on a funny face that someone's chalked out on the mat.

- to jump over a rope or magic string.

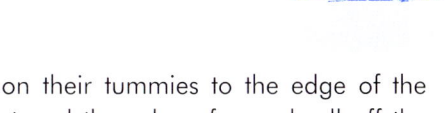

Really brave children can slide on their tummies to the edge of the table, put their hands on the mat and then do a forward roll off the table.

68

LARGE APPARATUS — MOVING SCENERY

The latest developments in leisure activities show quite clearly that we humans look for ways of testing the force of gravity and particularly enjoy moving in line with it or outside it.

When we balance, we can feel the tension problem between keeping and losing our balance. The better their balance is, the more safely and successfully children will move around and behave.

A sense of balance is a basic force which stimulates, regulates and integrates all our other senses, and, because it`s involved in steering all our movements, it must be trained again and again as it can otherwise quickly get out of practice.

BALANCING — IS EVERYTHING WELL-BALANCED?

Nina has just turned one and is starting to try to walk. She pulls herself up by the coffee table and tries to take two steps towards the nearest armchair. She manages to wobble her way across several times. Then she bravely has a go at another chair a bit further away but, despite repeated attempts, she doesn't succeed and keeps on landing on her well-padded Pampers-bottom.

The pull of the earth's gravity is the reason for many failed attempts at walking and lots of practice is needed until we humans can walk upright. The balancing centre in our ears, which reacts to the effect of the force of gravity and how we stand and change position, must be trained again and again, so that it learns to adapt to new and different situations.

Nicholas is three, so he can obviously not only walk well, but he can run and even stand on one leg. He can hardly pass a garden wall, without climbing onto it and balancing along the top. Every tree trunk in the woods has an irresistible pull to balance along that as well (much to his mother's chagrin, as she has to do the washing afterwards!); and yet this turns an otherwise normal woodland path into something much more challenging and interesting.

Nicholas likes riding his scooter and already has his first pair of roller skates. When he's a bit bigger, he'd like a bike and then he wants to learn to surf, and go skateboarding and snowboarding.

To get the hang of all these things in a playful way, Nina and Nicholas need a daily dose of "Balancing around and about", so that their bodies develop naturally and healthily. They'll need to put themselves into all sorts of new situations, which are even a bit daring on occasions.

Static Balance

You can feel static balance best when standing still. Because nobody can maintain his/her balance without tensing the supporting muscles and involving the whole body, the following exercises should be worked into every session, because they're indispensable for improving one's balance.

All the children run backwards and forwards across the hall to "running" music. Each time the music stops, they perform the following tasks, without wriggling or wobbling:

- freeze in the same position as when the music stopped.

- stop in a walking position but with your feet close together.

- stop and put your arms by your side.

- stop with your legs crossed.

- stop with your feet one in front of the other.

- stop and balance on the balls of your feet.

- stop again on the balls of your feet but crouching down.

- stay crouching down.

- stand on one leg.

- perform a trick (e. g. standing scales: one foot and two hands on the floor, one foot in the air.)

Dynamic Balance

"Dynamic" balance is felt whilst moving around and here you have a wide range of activities at your disposal of varying difficulty. What you offer the children must be clearly differentiated as "difficult" or "easy".

Easy

- wide base
- low construction
- all on one level
- fast walking/running
- short route
- firm and stable base
- flat ground
- move forwards
- seeing

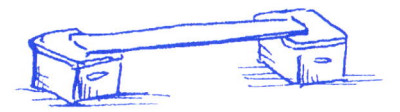

Difficult

- narrow base
- high construction
- slanting
- slow walking/running
- long route
- wobbly and unstable base
- uneven, wavy ground
- move backwards
- blindfolded

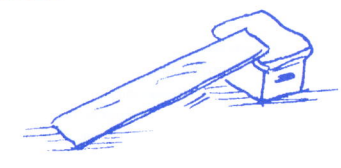

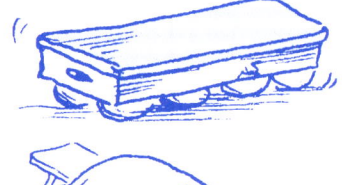

From Easy to Difficult

Lines Across the Hall

We'll now turn the lines on our sports hall floor into very narrow bridges which cross deep water, to give our children an increased sense of excitement and to challenge their imagination. So, watch out that you don't fall in, because there are hungry crocodiles and other dangerous animals down below.

The following exercises can be done on almost any sort of balancing apparatus and they can be transferred to all surfaces and levels of difficulty.

Let's run slowly or fast or on our own or in twos along all the different lines.

Low, stable apparatus

Seen from a motoric angle, balancing is a basic skill of co-ordination. On the one hand to extend one's co-ordination training and, on the other hand, to practise losing one's balance and then find it again, you can work with small pieces of apparatus, as follows:

- climb over medicine balls placed along a bench.

- walk along a bench in between dangling ropes.

- keep pushing a balloon into the air as you go.

- catch a ball which has been rolled towards you.

- catch a ball which has been thrown to you as you're balancing.

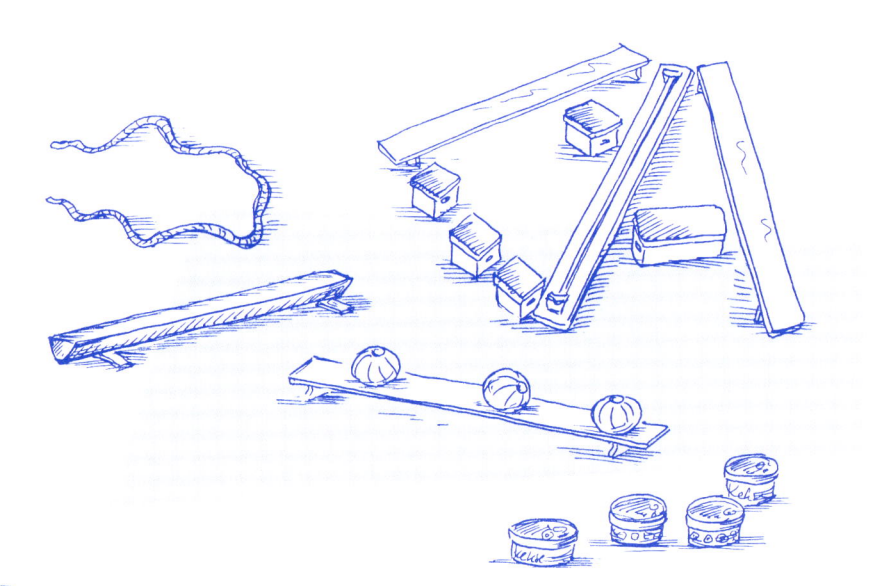

BALANCING AN OBJECT

- carry a bean bag on your head.

- carry a kitchen roll on the back of your hand.

- carry a gymnastics skittle on the palm of your hand.

- hold a building brick balanced on a beer mat without dropping it.

- let a table-tennis ball roll round a biscuit tin lid.

Movable apparatus

- run on a ball!

- sit on a ball, without touching the floor.

- lie on your tummy on a ball, without touching the floor.

- run, sit or lie on a cylindrical drum or roller.

- sit, lie or stand on a bench, whilst someone carefully turns it round.

THE HELPING POSITION

When you watch lots of groups, you will see that a firm hand from the leader doesn't let a child acquire a feeling of instability. A safety position which protects a child from falling and hurting itself is good but it's not so good to give a child too much support, thus preventing it from practising balancing for itself.

DIFFERENTIATION

Differentiation is especially suited to setting up balancing stages e. g. low and stable bridges next to bridges of medium height and then high, wobbly bridges. Each child can select its own particular challenge and move from easy to difficult, without any sense of failure.

SMALL GAMES

Children love playing and letting off steam and there's plenty of opportunity to do just that in our gymnastics sessions for small children. If you ask the children what they'd like to play, you usually get the same answer, and so it has become the custom in lots of groups to always play the same game at the end of each session.

These "rituals" play an important role in that they give the children a point of reference in each gymnastics session. They know that when this same game occurs, it's nearly time to go home. However, the group leader can keep on introducing new games, so that the children become familiar with different sorts of rules and tactical variations.

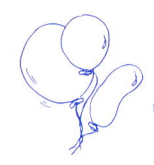

THE WASHING PEGS TOWER

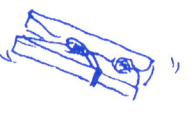

If we have a good look round where the washing machine is, the chances are that we'll come across a bag or bucket of pegs. We know only too well that little children like clipping pegs together to make a long snake, out of which we can make an object balancing game.

MATERIALS: 5 pegs per person

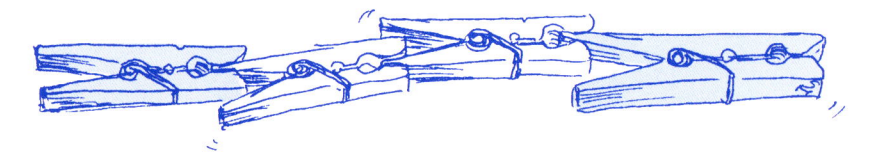

GAME IDEA 1:

Put lots of pegs on some soft floor covering in the middle of the hall. The children stand in a hoop about 2-3 metres away from the middle.

The game is played as follows:
All players start together. They each fetch two pegs and clip them together, then they run with this tiny tower back to their hoop, run round it once and go back to the middle to collect another peg for their tower. Do you think anyone can manage to fix 5 or more pegs together and still complete a run back to his/her hoop?

GAME IDEA 2:

All the children stand round the line of a circle with 2 or 3 pegs in front of them. One child starts building a tower out of 2 pegs, which is then passed on round the circle. Each child adds a peg until either no pegs remain or the tower collapses!

Egg Boxes

Someone really needs to have a good clearout up here in the box room! There are things lying around which surely aren't needed any more. Let's take all these old egg boxes into the sports hall because we've got a great game to play using tennis balls as well!

Materials: 1 egg box per 2 children
2-3 table-tennis balls, marbles or bouncy balls

Game idea:

Two children at a time kneel on the floor about 1 metre away from their egg box. They try and hit the hollows in the boxes with their table-tennis balls, their marbles or their bouncy balls. You can make it more interesting by painting the hollows and awarding different scores for each "hit".

Everyone plays against each other — everyone together

MATERIALS: Depending on the size of the group, one or more soft balls.

The aim of the game is to throw out a fellow player, but then to let him/her back into the game straight away.

All the children move about on a large playing area. The one with the ball tries to hit a fellow player. Children who've been hit sit on the floor. They are "freed" when they've got the ball in their hands. They can either get the ball themselves without moving from the spot, or a "freeing" ball can be rolled to them by another player. It goes without saying that you can't throw your "rescuer" out again immediately.

Fun Activities

While tidying up the house from the cellar to the loft, from the shed to the garage, we came across some useful items. A closer examination of these items made us think of the idea not only to invite children and moms or dads to the sportshall. So that is how it all started – the

Day out with the family in the land of the game inventors

On a Saturday afternoon or Sunday morning we are going to invite the whole family, mom, dad, grandma and grandpa, uncle, aunt, elder and younger siblings for our joint game-adventure.

It requires a bit of extra work to plan such a gymnastics session for the whole family, but actually, all you need to do is get a few things together and make them "suitable".

For the first half of the session you'll need:

> A LARGE NUMBER OF TABLE-TENNIS BALLS
> A REASONABLE AMOUNT OF PIPING
> (ABOUT 1 METRE LONG)
>
> CARDBOARD ROLLS
> (E.G. SAWN OFF ROLLS USED TO SELL CARPET ON AND WHICH YOU CAN FIND AT A CARPET WAREHOUSE)
>
> WASTE PIPES
> HERE YOU CAN USE SAWN-OFF WASTE PIPES, AVAILABLE FOR NOTHING, ESPECIALLY IF THE ENDS HAVE BEEN DAMAGED. ASK AT YOUR LOCAL D.I.Y. STORE.
>
> 2-3 ROLLS OF TOUGH STRING
>
> 2-3 PAIRS OF SCISSORS.
>
> 1 SMALL SAW

For the second half of the session you'll need:

> A FEW LORRY HOSES
>
> SEVERAL LONG PLANKS ABOUT 2.50 METRES LONG (E.G. INSULATING BOARD)
>
> WASTE PIPES
>
> POLYSTYRENE BLOCKS
>
> POSSIBLY 1 OR 2 LADDERS
>
> A FEW SKATEBOARDS (IF AVAILABLE)
>
> ALL THE APPARATUS YOU CAN FIND IN THE EQUIPMENT ROOM IN THE SPORTS HALL

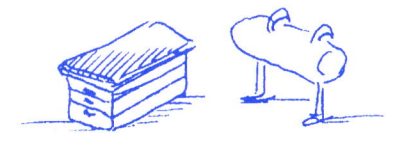

When you've got everything well prepared, the families can come, and we'll put them in the right mood for this special gymnastics session with the following story.

A DAY OUT WITH THE FAMILY IN THE LAND OF THE GAME INVENTORS

"I had actually invited lots of famous people today from the land of the game inventors, but unfortunately their manager rang me up this morning and told me that they're all ill and are lying in bed suffering from a highly infectious and puzzling cold.

Fortunately, they've already sent us various things in advance, which they wanted to invent some new games with. What do you think? Could we manage to invent lots of games and ideas for moving about, with all these cardboard rolls, balls and some string? Let's have a jolly good try! Pipes and waste pipes are divided out equally, together with little balls and a thick bundle of string. The children and their parents divide into groups and begin to experiment after which some families can present their initial results:

GAME INVENTION FROM THE IMAGINATIVE FAMILY

- push a pipe with your feet and roll it forwards

- 2 people roll a pipe backwards and forwards with their hands

- aim at a skittle with a pipe

- set a new record in long-distance rolling with a pipe

Game Invention from the Clever Family:

All members of the family kneel in a circle on the floor. Each of them holds a pipe down flat onto the floor with both hands. Using this as a "pusher", tennis balls are then pushed backwards and forwards across the circle.

Game Invention from the Fiddly Family:

- blow a table-tennis ball along the pipe

- pass a table-tennis ball from one pipe to the next

- put 2 pipes on end a short distance apart and then roll table-tennis balls through between the "goalposts".

Game Invention from the Handicraft Family:

- pull a piece of string through a pipe; two people hold the ends and let the pipe swing backwards and forwards, whilst other members of the family climb, jump or roll over the swaying pipe

- several pipes are fixed together to make one continuous surface, which makes a super massage bed.

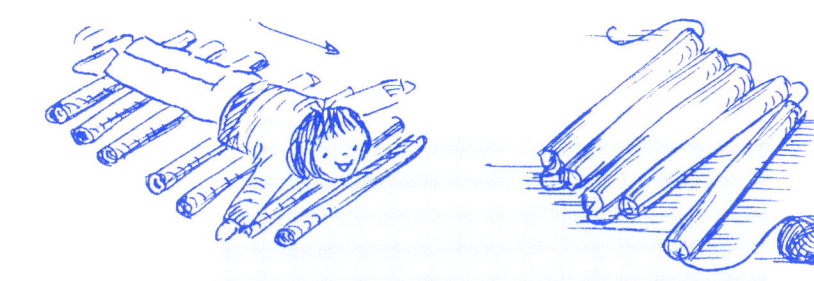

After a while, when everyone has tried out everyone elses's inventions, and the right sort of inventive spirit has been generated, nobody is surprised when everyone feels the urge to go to the land of the game inventors to pay them all a visit.

Everyone builds a big ship together with oars and a big sail and off they go:

After a long and troublesome journey with calm seas, hurricane winds, "child overboard plus a successful rescue operation...", everyone arrives safe and sound on the inventors' island. As soon as the ship had docked, the passengers stumbled, ran and hopped ashore, where lots of unusual things awaited them.

However, there was not a soul to be seen anywhere. But that didn't put them off, because they've brought their inventive spirit with them. Once they´d caught sight of planks, car tyres, polystyrene blocks etc., they had so many good ideas that they set to work immediately to transform the little island into a real play paradise.

ORGANISATIONAL TIPS:

It depends on the number of families taking part in this activity, whether they need to make a contribution to the necessary materials or whether everything is supplied free. So that no arguments arise, a good plan is to either draw lots amongst the players for the apparatus or play for it all. We'll now show you two ways that the families could "win" their carefully collected everyday materials. In addition, you can do what you like with all the big and small pieces of apparatus available to you in the sports hall. We'll leave it up to you to decide whether the families play on their own with their "won" materials, or whether they join forces with other families, thus giving themselves more freedom of choice. Ideally, everyone comes together towards the end and builds a big play island for everyone to investigate.

1. PLAYING CARDS:

We need to write a card for everything we find in the garage (lorry hoses, planks, ladders, drain pipes etc.) and then put all the cards face down on the floor. The families each choose 3-4 cards and build their movable island with the appropriate apparatus.

2. THIMBLE OR "LITTLE HATS" GAME:

Using a see-saw, yoghurt pots or bean bags are then flicked onto the squares of a marked out "board" (e.g. 3+3). You first need to stabilize the pots with a bit of melted wax poured into each of them. In each square of the "board" you'll find cards with the named pieces of apparatus which you've "won". You can vary your number of attempts according to the amount of available apparatus and the families playing.

CREATIVE CORNER

A CHILD'S SNUGGLY CUSHION COSTUME

MATERIALS:
bright material (old bed sheets or duvet covers), elastic (2 cm wide), bias binding, paints suitable for painting material, stencils for the sun, moon, stars, clouds or any other desired motif.

HOW TO MAKE YOUR COSTUME:
Squares of material 30x30 cm are cut out for the back and front and the edges finished off on the sewing machine or with bias binding, leaving 2 ends of the binding 25 cm longer as ties. The two sections are then fixed together with 2 strips of 16 cm elastic, and sewn 5 cm in from the edge.

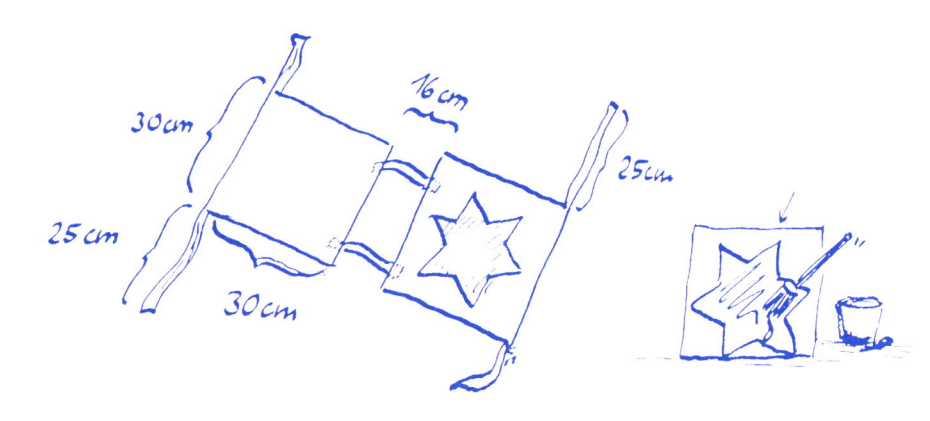

PAINTING:
You can paint your chosen motifs onto the material using the stencils. Then, depending on the colour, everything needs to be "fixed" i.e. ironed.

Notes:

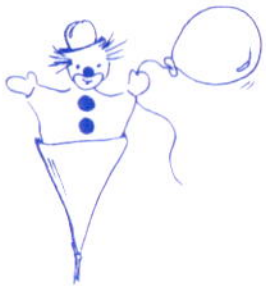

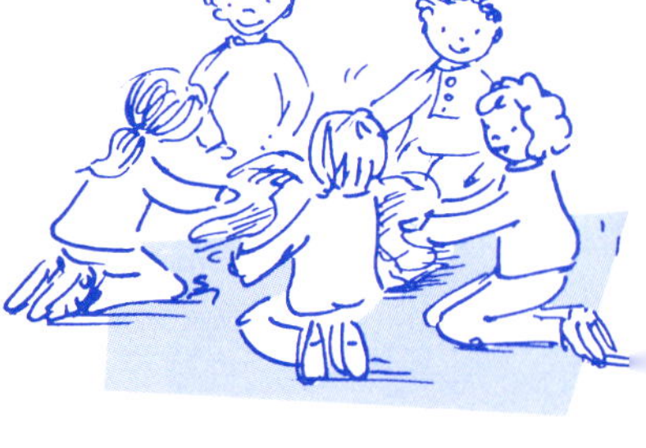